HIGHWAYS IN THE BYWAYS

I rode forth, if not like the knights of old, at any rate as one eager upon his quest and prepared to find a thrill in every mile of the way.

HIGHWAYS IN THE BYWAYS

The Story of a Pilgrimage in
John Wesley's Steps

BY

LESLIE A. NEWMAN, F.R.G.S.

THE EPWORTH PRESS
(EDGAR C. BARTON)
25–35 City Road, London, E.C.1

First published 1944
Second impression 1945

THIS BOOK IS PRODUCED IN COMPLETE CONFORMITY WITH THE AUTHORIZED ECONOMY STANDARDS

PRINTED IN GREAT BRITAIN
BY WESTERN PRINTING SERVICES LTD., BRISTOL

CONTENTS

PART ONE

THE MOORS

PART TWO

THE DALES

PART THREE

THE WOLDS

FOREWORD

Two years ago, with some misgiving, I allowed a journalist to tell the story of my adventures on horseback. I had the feeling that the theme was so intimate and private that it would be better unrecorded. Now, to my surprise, I find myself writing a book of that adventure. The goodwill of my friends, and also the many requests I have had to give the story both on the platform and in this more permanent form, have brought about this reorientation.

A very special debt of gratitude is acknowledged to my friends, John Ventress and H. L. Gee, without whose help both the journey and this record would have been impossible, and without whose friendship my life would be impoverished.

LESLIE A. NEWMAN

The Methodist Central Hall
Queen Street
Scarborough

Love's in the highroad,
Love's in the byroad—
Love's in the meadow, and
Love's in the mart;
And down every byway
Where I've taken my way,
I've met love a-smiling—for
Love's in my heart.

DANA BURNET

PART ONE

THE MOORS

LEAPING into the saddle, I patted my horse. I waved 'Good-bye' to my friends, and rode off, bound upon a happy adventure.

Few men, I think, enjoy the routine of the ministry more than I, for I have no quarrel with the common round and daily task, both glorious because a part of His service. But setting out that memorable morning, sitting astride a fine, strong horse, leaving the familiar and facing new scenes and new possibilities, all this gave me a feeling of exhilaration, and I rode forth, if not like the knights of old, at any rate as one eager upon his quest and quite prepared to find a thrill in every mile of the way.

I remember how sweet that morning seemed, how fair the Yorkshire countryside as I rode between the moors and the sea. I remember the music of my horse's hoofs, the very smell and strength and cleanness of him. I remember the motion of the saddle, and the joy of 'looking down' on folk we passed, not (I trust) because I was condescending, but because they smiled when they looked up at me! And so, without haste, we left the town behind, saw the last red roofs drop behind the hill, found the heather all about us—purple against a blue and sunny sea—and fell in love with adventure from the first.

Our first day was uneventful, and during the ride northwards from Scarborough I had ample time in which to meditate. There was, I must confess, a little heart-searching, and more than once I kept asking myself how it came about that instead of the ordinary duties of a minister I was, that bright morning, in the saddle.

HOW IT BEGAN

Where was I going? *Why* was I going?

The questions constantly recurred. What had prompted me to ride abroad on horseback in an age of motor-cars—not to mention army lorries and tanks?

My mind went back to a wet afternoon in Bristol, and as I jogged along in the North I recalled a great experience of the South that day I had first stood before the equestrian statue of John Wesley. The strikingly lifelike sculpture had stirred me deeply, so much so that for a long time I stood there oblivious to the rain. How truly the sculptor had caught the very spirit of the little man astride that gallant steed; and how finely, too, he had portrayed the horse, no mere dumb creature, but rather a being alert and aware, anxious to be off upon his mission, agog to take the high road or the low road in a great piece of service. As for the figure of John Wesley, it reminded me that he, surely, was one of the greatest horsemen of all time. Though not robust, he travelled no less than 5,000 miles a year for over half the eighteenth century, a total of 250,000 miles, or the equivalent of ten times round the earth. And he did it in an age when the best roads were worse than all but our worst to-day; yet the little man who founded Methodism thought nothing of mounting a horse in London, riding to Scotland, returning along the west coast to Bristol, and so to London again. And all the time (as I remembered that sunny morning) the tireless clergymen with the auburn hair flowing in the breeze was not merely the best-known traveller on the roads of eighteenth-century England, but the most welcome of all, for once men and women realized what his mission was they flocked to see him and to hear him. Everywhere he travelled, not for the love of travelling, but with a mighty purpose in his heart, proclaiming to a lonely man or a vast multitude the unsearchable riches of Christ.

That first day's ride took me close by Robin Hood's Bay which, I reflected, John Wesley had visited no less than a dozen times, often in spite of blizzards and snowdrifts, always counting the little, remote spot worthy of his attention, deserving of his affection. So too, when I came over the brow of the hill and looked down upon the ancient town of Whitby, I thought again of John Wesley; and when I cantered through the narrow streets and came to the chapel in which he preached I felt indeed that if, greatly daring and perhaps presuming more than I ought, I could ride where John Wesley had ridden, and try, in all humility, to preach as and when and where John Wesley had preached, I might do something worth doing.

This, then, was a part, but only a part, of my motive for taking to the saddle. Shortage of petrol may have been a contributory factor. A novel holiday may have been another. Love of adventure, I dare say, helped to urge me on. But more than these was my desire to try out Wesley's eighteenth-century methods in this twentieth century—an experiment in evangelism, I suppose.

Yet all this was not the beginning and end of my 800 miles in Yorkshire. There was something else. There was a deep yearning to meet men and women on the road of life, to come unexpectedly upon opportunities for service, to preach in the villages, to let the spaciousness of the outdoor world sink into and enlarge my own soul and experience: and, finally and in a word, to do, as best I could, something of what an even greater traveller than John Wesley tried to do. I thought, at the very outset of my pilgrimage on horseback, of those trenchant words of St. Paul:

> And I, brethren, when I came unto you, came not with excellency of speech or of wisdom, proclaiming to you the mystery of God. For I determined not to know anything among you, save Jesus Christ, and Him crucified. And I was with you in weakness, and in fear, and in much trembling. And my speech and my preaching were not in persuasive words of wisdom, but in demonstration of the Spirit and of power: that your faith should not stand in the wisdom of men, but in the power of God.

There, truly, was the motive and meaning, the purpose and persuasion of my journey. As I mused on my motives and rode along I knew that, however imperfectly and unworthily these words were echoed in my heart, this alone must be the purpose and the spirit of my adventure.

DICK TURPIN

I ought, I think, to say at least a word or two about my horse—without whom, in wartime, my journey might have become merely a cycling tour, or have dwindled to the proportions of a pilgrimage on shoe leather.

Finding a horse to carry me so many hundreds of miles, most of them across trackless country or along rough lanes, might have been an extraordinarily hard task but for a good friend of mine, a farmer who has never failed me. He knew just the mount for me, he assured me, and I doubt if I could have found a better had I searched the world. A truly noble creature, he had run so magnificently before the war that he had forty prizes to his credit. He was all that a horse should be, strong and tough and determined, yet docile and faithful. He moved with an easy grace and a proud bearing, and from the first there was mutual understanding between us—an all-important factor in riding. I may say that in spite of the miles this horse covered, he returned in even better form than he set out, for everywhere he was admired, and all who admired him were ready to provide the best food and shelter.

His name was Dick Turpin.

A few of my friends whispered that they thought it odd that Dick Turpin and John Wesley should be linked together by my pilgrimage, yet the farther I travelled on the back of the one in the steps of the other the more certain I became that the combination was excellent. I reflected in the first few miles that if only to-day the Church could link the audacity of that bold Yorkshire highwayman, Dick Turpin, with the spiritual vision and lofty mission of John Wesley, tremendous things might happen for the kingdom of God. Sitting in the saddle, Dick Turpin between my knees, I became as the adventure continued something of a highwayman myself, my objective the souls of men and women rather than the finery on their fingers.

So, as I say, I set out from Scarborough, rode beyond Robin Hood's Bay and Whitby, turned inland, and cantered downhill and up again to the shy hamlet of Littlebeck. I think I was led by the Spirit to that spot, for there in the evening of my first day in the saddle I had fellowship with one of the grand old men of Methodism. He welcomed me. He talked with me. He saw, more clearly than I had done, the immense possibilities of my adventure. Father of the village (as the folk thereabouts affectionately call him), he prayed for me . . . and it is not surprising, therefore, that things began to happen the next day!

THE TANKS

It was a glorious morning as Dick Turpin picked his way cautiously across the Whitby Moors. On all sides were patches of purple heather mingled with emerald, all drenched with sunshine. John Wesley (I recalled) had often travelled that road, and knew it intimately, yet on this morning we saw two things he had never seen. Everywhere we came upon huge, ugly bomb-craters, unsightly wounds among the heather. An old postman told me that as he went his rounds across the moors he passed over three hundred of them. One dark night some two years earlier the Luftwaffe, mistaking a moorland fire for an important target, had spent a whole night emptying their bombs upon it. Bombs destroying the beauty! What would Wesley have thought?

Moreover, we were constantly startled by tanks which came rushing out at us from the most unexpected places, swinging round some hidden corner, or leaping up out of a crater. The Tank Corps was practising in deadly earnest. Dick violently objected to these iron steeds, and I had some awkward moments. When we came to a stationary tank it seemed a good opportunity to cure him of his fear of them. Slowly, therefore, and cautiously, prompted by much urging, he approached the strange object, but as we advanced, the turret flew open, and out popped the perspiring head of a young American. Dick, of course, backed; but when I finally coaxed him near again, the laughing young man in the tank and the man on the horse had a chance to get acquainted.

'Is it very hot in there?' I asked.

'Hot?' he ejaculated. 'Hot! Scorching, red hot! Hot as hell!'

'H'm, that's a hot spot, you know.'

'Have you ever lived there?' he challenged with a grin.

'No, but I know a man who is living there now.'

Then I told him of some one to whom I had spoken a few hours before, some one whose mind was aflame with evil desires and whose heart was burning with foul passions. 'Hell is a very real experience,' I added.

I fancy both of us enjoyed crossing verbal swords. There were smiles and laughter on both sides, yet before I left that boy I had an opportunity of saying something which may have given him a new idea about the hideousness of evil. The fact that he said, 'This has been a devilishly good chat', did not detract from its value.

Why do we always think that big things can only be discussed in a solemn and often artificial manner? Often it is much more our *manner* than our *matter* which folk resent, and I have a notion that many a man would listen if we were more human and humorous in our approach.

Tanks and bombs! What would Wesley have made of them? His eighteenth-century world was different, of course; but my mind was toying with this question as we trotted on, Dick and I, when, like a flash, the answer came. Would he not have regarded them in much the same way as he did bear-baiting and cock-fighting in his own day? These were but the modern symptoms of the old fundamental disease. The outward expressions of sin may change, but the old enemy is still our most insidious foe.

Rievaulx Abbey

Scagglesthorpe Chapel

FRIENDS IN NEED

Shortly after this I had occasion to be very grateful to the Tank Corps. Passing through Troutsdale, we encountered an experience which might easily have ended the whole adventure. Having carefully closed a gate and travelled about a third of the way across a spacious field, we became surrounded by a number of wild horses. They galloped round us in an ever-closing circle, making several unpleasant attempts to close in. One very handsome but ugly-spirited creature galloped in front, and then lashed out with her hind legs, catching Dick full on the shoulder. Fortunately, she did not seriously injure him. Meanwhile, the horses were mustering for another attack. The position was grim, when two tanks came charging across the field, driving our assailants before them. Never have I been more thankful for the British Army, and never happier to clear a gate and reach the security of the other side.

This encounter had taken me off the beaten track, and an hour or so later Dick and I found ourselves on a roadless, deserted part of the moor. We wandered on until a farm came into view. Clattering into the yard, I was about to ask for guidance when the farmer's wife called out: 'Would you like a glass of milk?'

The words were music, but before I could answer, out came the farmer himself.

'You'll be Mr. Newman,' he said. 'I'm just reading about you in the *Christian Herald*. Come on, now, give the horse a rest, and step in and join us at tea.'

The genuine pleasure and the great kindness of these complete strangers was as deeply refreshing as it was unexpected. Friends in need on the roadways of life! Those who anticipate our needs and always suggest the extra milk—not water! How much we owe to them. These two were but typical of scores of such families I met all along the way.

To have accepted their invitation to stay an hour or two would have been delightful, but a horse has only four speeds—walk, trot, canter, gallop—and these cannot be used like the speeds of a car. Time was pressing. So, across a few fields, down the steepest of steep hills, and we were in the lovely valley of Ellerburn, a most enchanting place.

EVENSONG IN ELLERBURN

As we trotted alongside a gurgling stream we heard in the distance the sound of church bells calling folk to an unusual weekday service, and presently we came to a small Saxon church. It was altogether off the beaten track, a place of worship amid scenery that stirred the heart with its grandeur. Two Anglican vicars were awaiting me at the gate, and it was a joy to find that this small church, which holds about a hundred folk and is some miles from the nearest village, was full. During the simplified form of Evensong the vicar paid sincere tributes to the Wesleys and their work, suggesting that the primary need of our day is that all the churches should lay emphasis upon evangelism. To worship in Ellerburn's church without feeling its historic importance is impossible. From Saxon times Christians have worshipped here, and in this green valley there was but one subject on which to speak, namely, the Love of God to which this spot had borne witness through so many years. It was an unforgettable privilege to address that appreciative congregation.

While speaking of my indebtedness to members of other churches than my own it might be well to explain that one of the purposes of my journey was to foster co-operation between the different branches of the Universal Church.

The story of what happened at Sinnington, for example, is typical. Arriving in this village with its green, its mass of foliage, and its musical stream, I found that, thanks to one of my colleagues, a large company had assembled. Ominous clouds, however, compelled us to retire to the chapel. Sitting at the front was a man whose identity it would have been difficult to detect. He wore a sports jacket, plus-fours, and a very distinctive tie. All through the service he listened in that helpful way known to all speakers, and afterwards, while I spoke to others, he lingered on. Then he came up and said, 'I'm the vicar of this place, and I'm most interested in what you are doing. If you would speak for us in the parish church I should love to share another service with you.'

My heart warmed to this kindly man. How different the treatment he showed me from that meted out to John Wesley by the Established Church of his day! The number of people at this subsequent service was a high tribute to this generous and large-minded vicar.

Before leaving the village of Sinnington I cannot refrain from recalling an odd fishing incident. Trout are fairly plentiful in the stream, and on the morning of the day I arrived, an expert angler had provided himself with a new outfit. He had a new rod and line, new hooks and flies, and some new waders. After flicking his flies for about two hours and catching nothing he was joined by a small boy. This lad had only a stick and a piece of string with a pin and worm attached. He began operations about two yards from the expert, and in less than fifteen minutes had pulled out a large fish. The angler was annoyed, and straightway began fishing where the boy had pulled out his prize, but he caught nothing. Although I did not stay to confirm what happened, I was later told that during the morning the boy caught three trout, the expert none. As Dick and I trotted away from that village stream the thought running through my mind was—well, you know what it was. Who was it who said, 'I will make you to become fishers of men'? It seems that one needs more than good equipment. It is possible, surely, to have a perfect organization, with machinery that has been designed to do the very work required, and yet still to fail. Blest is he who has the instinct that can tell when and where to fish in the waters of life. His unconscious technique will accomplish what the mere technician can never do. In all matters that affect life, good men will work a bad machine better than bad men will work a good machine. The personal factor is more important than the impersonal factory.

UP AND DOWN

The next stage of my journey took me among the hill villages. Between these villages are deep dales which often involve long journeys to places actually quite near. While passing through one of these villages, Thornton-le-dale, I met a most humorous person. His quiet, expressionless face and his plain, workaday clothes would never have led one to suspect the true nature of this practical joker.

It came about like this: I had already inquired from several villagers as to where I should find the burial-place of Matthew Grimes. Forgetting how short is human memory, I had imagined that every one would know of the man who had once guarded Napoleon, and who had eventually been chosen to help to carry him to his grave. Most of them, however, looked at me in astonishment and asked, 'Who is he?' (This is the more surprising as his grave is quite distinctive, and contains a record of the many deeds of a worthy son of the village.) But at length I encountered a man with a keen sense of humour.

Having intrigued me into asking about his work he said, 'Oh, I'm in charge of about 30,000 people'.

I whistled. 'Oh!' I exclaimed, 'you'll be the mayor of some town?'

'No. But I'm looking after the most democratic crowd in the world. We have men and women on equal terms. Our rich and poor are so mixed up that riches make no difference. I never have the slightest trouble with any of them, although they represent every shade of political and religious difference. Never once have I had any bother, for in my firm all share alike.' All this time he had looked profoundly serious. Then, after a long pause he added, 'It was decided that there should be only *one* test for any one joining the firm'.

'What was that?'

'Character, if they square on *that* no other questions are asked.'

'But', I said, 'this is the Utopia for which the world is waiting. And you have thirty thousand such people under you?'

'Yes.'

'Then what are you?'

'A cemetery attendant!'

Bad taste or not, it was impossible not to laugh at his thoughts about the democracy of death; and as my horse trotted up the road to Lockton I noticed that the countryman's sombre face was now wrinkled in a great grin.

Looking at the Lockton area one gets the impression that some vast giant has clawed out five valleys with his massive fingers, and that the fairies of beauty had covered up his rude work with their finest art. Up and down, and down and up, we moved among country almost as thrilling as the Rockies. Just beyond Levisham station I was confronted with the alternative of either taking a long way round by road or clambering up what the local people call the 'bankside', and what, in reality, is the precipitous side of a mountain. I chose the short cut—and never did a short cut prove such a long way round. Up this trackless height we were toiling, Dick struggling hard to keep his feet, and I clinging to the saddle in preparation to dismount, when, snap, the girth burst asunder. Down came the saddle and down fell the rider! Over and over I rolled. Oh, what a fall was there! Yet, having reached an unkind resting-place I found myself longing to inform Hitler that short cuts often lead to downfalls. From previous experience I knew what it was like to be thrown over a horse's head, but never before had I rolled over its hindquarters. Let it be said to the credit of this amazing old horse that he immediately stopped, looked round in amazement blended with sympathy, and then came quietly down to help. How we eventually struggled to the top and continued the journey can be better imagined than told.

THE MAN ON FIRE

When Wesley came riding through these dale villages he must often have longed to stay, for there are few places of such peace and beauty. It is as though Nature has selected these little valleys with the express purpose of hiding some of her richest treasures. Such a treasure is Lastingham. It would be a crime not to dismount at this spot for a moment.

Here I was met by a friend who said he wished to show me something. I followed him to the village church, tied up my horse, and went within. In the centre of the nave is a flight of steps leading down to one of the most interesting crypts to be found anywhere. Built in the sixth century, it is so well preserved that it might have been created yesterday.

Opening the door, I was so gripped by the scene that for a time I could not move. I looked in wonder. At each side were huge square pillars which seemed to be holding up the church above, and at the far end, above a tiny altar, a window let in the daylight. This made a halo round an ancient cross and sent its shadow across the crypt. Instinctively one is quiet.

'What do you think of it?' asked my guide presently.

'It's like peeping down the centuries,' I whispered.

'Yes,' he said, as he looked at the pillars and the shadow along the floor, '*it makes one sure of the strength and permanence of the Christian truth.*'

If ever I am tempted to think that the philosophies and crudities of a few decades like these through which we are passing can overturn the truth of the Gospel, I shall visit Lastingham and look into this crypt. Those massive pillars upholding the church and the brooding shadow of Love's symbol will take me quickly to the things that abide.

But this was not what my friend had really brought me to see, for presently he directed me to a small plaque outside the church. It told how, near to that spot, John Foster lay in peace, gallant John Foster, one of Wesley's early rider-preachers. He was born in this quiet village, and after meeting Wesley he went up and down the country like a flame of fire. For five years, said the inscription, he did this, *and then burnt out.*

Burnt out! My mind rebelled. He did not. He could not. John Foster was one of those who set the kingdom ablaze, and counted not his life dear unto himself; and such a man does not burn out when he hands on the flame to others. *He distributes himself.* There are many in the country to-day who owe their spiritual life to John Foster, and he is more alive now than many who are not dead!

'Oh, that all might catch the flame,
All partake the glorious bliss!'

Standing in front of that simple plaque, thinking of this man and the work he did, reflecting on the need of our present age for just such men as he, I could do one thing only. I bowed my head. I prayed that God would raise up more men like John Foster. Neither my friend nor I had spoken a word, but when I glanced at my companion I saw that his head was bowed too. I am sure you would have done the same.

FOR OF SUCH . . .

At Hutton-le-Hole one is in a dream-village.

Not without good cause does it claim to be one of the prettiest villages in Yorkshire. With its stream cutting out pictures in the rocks, its quaint, trim, little houses on either side of the long and spacious green, and with the wide-embracing moorland stretching out arms of beauty on every side, it is a delight.

Dick was grazing on the village green while I reclined on a seat, eating my lunch, when presently a small boy approached. He was perhaps six. Keeping a fair distance between himself and my horse he went around, his eyes wide open in wonder. Then he sidled up timidly and asked, 'Mister, does he bite?'

'No, he doesn't bite, at least not little boys.'

I watched him as again he considered the horse with the eye of a young connoisseur, and then came back with the query: 'Mister does he kick?'

'No, he won't kick,' I assured him.

Yet a third time he inspected Dick Turpin. Finally came the revelation of what he really wanted. 'Mister,' he begged, 'I should like a ride.'

'You would? All right, you shall have one,' I declared.

So I picked him up, placed him in the saddle, and started walking Dick around the green.

The result was amazing. Soon all the children in the neighbourhood seemed to have collected. They were hoping for a ride, but I was seeking a congregation, and it was not long before I found one. The simple idea had never occurred to me that the children could be drawn together by the horse himself. How those youngsters listened while we thought of the story of Dick Turpin the highwayman, then of the story of this horse that was named after him, and after that of what he was now attempting to do. Little by little the boys and girls were led on to the story of the Great Horseman who loved children. They knew who was meant when I told them that one day He had ridden an untamed colt through a crowd of people and cheering children into an Eastern city. There is, I believe, behind the Palm Sunday story the evidence that Jesus really was a great horseman, for it was no mean feat to ride an unsaddled horse, *on which no man had previously ridden*, through an excited Eastern crowd.

Since that first accidental discovery of a way in which children could be attracted, Dick gathered crowds on scores of village greens. He rarely failed, and I think of him now as a missionary and evangelist!

NOT FOR SALE

Not only children but adults too were brought to me by the horse. Thus, not long after the incident at Hutton-le-Hole we were cantering along the verge of a road when a car passed by. Presently it stopped, turned, and was driven back. Out stepped a typical Yorkshire farmer, and after looking critically at Dick for a few minutes, he said:

'How much do you want for him?'

I gasped, and said, 'Do you want to buy him?'

'Aye, I could do with one like that,' he declared.

'Sorry,' I replied, 'he's not for sale. I'll tell you what I'm doing, though, I'm giving something away!'

He looked at me uncertainly. Clearly he thought me mad. I went on to say that all the best things in life are free—air, beauty, hope, love, and so on. I reminded him that all these were gifts. Then I said that God always gives things and that He never sells them. 'The gift of God's forgiveness', I said, 'is something we may have if we will receive it. It cannot be earned or bought, but we may ask and receive.'

He stood there by the roadside listening patiently, giving no clue as to what he was thinking. By his parting words I felt sure that he was not one who went to church very often. 'Well, maybe you're right,' he said. 'Anyhow, go on and tell some more folks —and good luck.'

Without another word he drove off. I was not altogether dissatisfied, for the seed had been sown in the mind of a farmer, and I would as soon sow seeds there as anywhere. Unlike so many of us who live in towns and find our minds preoccupied with many things, the countryman ponders long and deliberately over what he hears. There is no more fertile soil for seeds of truth than the mind of a farmer. This leads me on to speak of some of the most remarkable people I have met.

FARMERS OF FARNDALE

Farndale, when the wild daffodils make it a sea of gold, is a sight never to be forgotten, a choice gift of our English countryside at its best. The people of this beauty spot are as unspoiled as their dale. Never in my wanderings have I found anything more like eighteenth-century England than here among the old-fashioned places and people of Farndale. Let me introduce you to a character whose type is rarely met with in these days.

Fifteen minutes, at most, was all I had been in the dale when I first met Amos. This sturdy man of medium height, with his bronzed smiling face and uprolled sleeves, I shall never forget. Like his Biblical namesake he is a son of the soil, and has worked on the land of his forebears all his life. With the native caution characteristic of this region he spent some thirty minutes making sure of me, and then said, 'I'd like to show you something. Would you care for a climb?'

So, having put Dick Turpin in one of his fields, we started off up the steep side of Bracken Edge. I dare say we climbed some two hundred feet, and all that time Amos gave me no clue as to his intention. In my own mind I had concluded that he was going to show me one of the many enchanting views of Farndale—and surely there are few outside Paradise to surpass them. Suddenly, however, when we were near the top, he stopped and pointed to a patch of purple heather.

'It happened there,' he said.

'What happened there?' I asked, puzzled.

'It will be near forty year since it happened there,' he repeated.

'Yes, but what?'

Then he explained that as a young man he had been unhappy for two years. His depression deepened until one morning he and his dog were at this spot. He felt so oppressed that he could not take another step forward.

'I was arrested and rooted here,' were his words. 'In those days we called it conviction of sin, but you moderns wouldn't know the meaning of *that*,' he added significantly. 'I knew, though. I went down on my knees. I prayed. I prayed and wept until, finally, God lifted the load and the light came. Then I leapt for joy, and ran triumphantly down the hillside with a song in my heart. God has kept me singing ever since.'

Perhaps in print this does not seem impressive, but I was deeply moved. There, on that height, it was like hearing St. Paul give his version of what happened on the Damascus road.

So intrigued was I that later I made extensive inquiries about this unusual character, Amos. First, I asked an old man in the valley if he knew anything about that happening which long years before had changed a life.

'Aye, I remember it well,' he told me. 'We *knew* it was going to happen.'

Mystified, I said, 'You knew it was going to happen? But how?'

'Well, for the two years Amos was under conviction, a few of us were meeting each night and praying for him. We prayed for him definitely, and by name, *just for him*. We *knew* it would happen and were not surprised when, after we'd been praying all that time, it did happen. He came one Sunday and told us all about it!'

Think of it! For two years nightly they had prayed, personally, definitely, specifically, never doubting prayer would work a miracle! When I heard of it I wondered if one of the reasons why so few things happen now is because we do not expect them. If only we loved our fellows enough to do that!

From others I learned that Amos is to-day one of the best-known and most respected people in the dale. If any one is ill it is for Amos folk send. If any one dies it is often Amos who takes the parting service. For forty years he has been like this and it all started on the top of Bracken Edge where he met God.

That night I was speaking in the little church where Amos worships, and in the course of the address, quite casually and without any great expectations, I remarked: 'Now, supposing you were eighteenth-century people, and that the real John Wesley came to share a service with you, do you know what he would say? He would say: "To-morrow morning, before I continue my journey and you go to your fields, we shall have a service, and I'll be here at five o'clock!" What,' I asked, 'would you think if I made such a suggestion nowadays?'

Amos was sitting just to my right. The suggestion proved too much for him.

'You try us!' he exclaimed.

Rarely have I known anything so glorious as the next morning. I remember catching Dick Turpin in a dark field. I remember cantering two miles down to the little chapel as the sun rose over the edge of the moor. I remember that the music of the dawn was the clattering of hoofs and the singing of the birds. I remember how the promise of a new day thrilled me. Yet it must be confessed that in my mind was an unworthy thought. I could not help wondering if the people would come. I knew how much easier it is to promise at night than to resist the appeal of one's bed early in the morning. Had I known Farndale folk better I should not have worried; and when I reached the chapel I found not only those who had promised, but others too. And what a thrill that early morning service was! After our praise and prayer together we shared some thoughts about growth in Grace, and the fullness of life, and finally, while the sun was still low in the sky, we gathered in a circle in the heart of the village and sang morning hymns of gladness. Many of the men in the congregation belonged to a male voice choir, and their unaccompanied singing was beyond the power of words to describe. Even now that music still echoes in my mind.

As Dick and I picked our way up the steep road out of the valley I was thinking how much Methodists had lost since they discontinued their early morning services. Nowadays, when the clock is one hour before noon, folk will sing 'Early in the morning our songs shall rise to Thee!' I shall never sing that at eleven again without feeling that Farndale is laughing at me. Then I wondered if our ready assumptions about the indifference of this age were really sound. How readily and spontaneously these folk had responded! Was it only the novelty? Was it a survival of interest from the past or a sign that people to-day are longing for God? Would the idea work elsewhere? I can only say that I have since made the suggestion in numbers of places and never once without response. Slowly I have come to feel that the age is not indifferent. Different, of course, different in a thousand ways, but not indifferent. We are still hungry for reality.

When my horse and I reached the top of the valley and came to the gracious little church at Gillamoor I noticed that some one had placed on the church wall a plaque bearing an inscription—one of John Keble's verses:

Thou who hast given me eyes to see
And love this sight so fair,
Give me a heart to find out Thee,
And read Thee everywhere.

Looking back over Farndale from this vantage spot, known as the Surprise View, I felt how utterly appropriate these words were, not merely to that panorama of Nature's wonderland, but to some of the finest folk I have ever met, the Farndale farmers.

Fadmoor, which almost joins Gillamoor, gave me a good opportunity of trying out the new things I had learned, and here again the witness of song on the village green, and early morning service, were features not soon forgotten. The small chapel proved to be the right size for the afternoon service, but in the evening we found it necessary to take possession of the village hall. This, too, was crowded by folk anxious, it seemed, to hear a message on *The Allies' Secret Weapon.*

Every horseman in the land would have envied me my ride the next morning, for it took me through some of the loveliest scenery in Yorkshire, far off the beaten track through Sleightholmdale and Pockley, and on through Riccaldale. Clambering up towering heights, riding among forest trees, or wading across deep and rushing streams, I went. Riding in the Wild West offers nothing better, I imagine, and Dick revelled in it. He seemed to know that my own mind was aglow with something besides the beauties around, for that afternoon we were to have a service in the historic Abbey at Rievaulx. About two miles from this objective we were invited to lunch at a kindly farm, where, after the meal, a number of us gathered in the farm-kitchen for prayer, a preparation for the service which was to follow.

RIEVAULX RESURRECTED

The first sight of Rievaulx Abbey from the hill-tops is thrilling. It looks like a beautifully carved jewel in a green setting. I am not surprised that Dorothy Wordsworth was held speechless by it, and that Turner spent hours trying to capture its elusive loveliness on canvas. As we drew further down the hill we saw the waiting company waving their hands while we were yet afar off. The occasion was unique, for never before had a Methodist service been held in this hallowed spot, a poem in stone, and I gladly express my gratitude to the Office of Works for so readily granting permission. Chairs were arranged in the old choir, and standing before what had once been the High Altar I shared in one of the most memorable services I had ever known. All our hearts were stirred to be on that sacred soil. Perhaps it is not unfitting to put on record a few comments about this remarkable service. How the crowd gloried in the opening hymn of praise, 'Hail, Thou once despised Jesus!' How they listened as a quartet sang, 'Come, sinners, to the gospel feast' to the tune of 'Rievaulx'! How the voices throbbed under those vast, majestic arches, where for hundreds of years the monastic choir had sung! Standing in that venerable ruin, drenched with the sanctuary songs of the past, it seemed not inappropriate to speak about the first three Christian songs: The *Magnificat* (song of the heart), the *Benedictus* (song of the home and homeland), and the *Nunc Dimittis* (song of the world).

Together we remembered how these had so often been sung within Rievaulx's sacred walls.

The old keeper of Rievaulx told me a lovely story. In response to my query as to whether there were any ghosts thereabouts, he said, 'Yes! I've seen them!'

Then he went on to describe how, one moonlight night, he was awakened by singing in the Abbey. Peering from his window, he saw figures flitting about the choir. It was all queer, unearthly. Determined to get to the bottom of the mystery, he had gone down from his cottage and cautiously and wonderingly approached the ruin. Figures of nuns, it seemed, were moving here and there, the dead restored to life; and he realized at once that they were engaged in some form of service. At last he cried out in a loud voice, 'Hi, there! Who are you? What are you doing?' Instead of the figures vanishing, however, they surrounded him. They were no tenuous forms, but flesh and blood—nuns who had come over from Helmsley, near by, to hold a special service on a saint's day—and without permission. He knew of no other ghosts, and chuckled as he remarked, 'All Rievaulx's ghosts are real 'uns.'

I had little time to ride to Coxwold for an evening meeting, but Dick knew his job, and never travelled better. Indeed, I managed in between the gallops to have a word with some soldiers on the moors, some children in the village of Wass, and a good look at Byland Abbey, a spot which makes a wonderful study for both the antiquarian and the student of Christian history. Its massive proportions are still clearly outlined, though it is not in such a good state of preservation as Rievaulx.

SHANDY'S GHOST

Coxwold need apologize to no village in England. It is exquisite. Its long, broad street and wide grass verges, its quaint old stone houses, and strikingly handsome octagonal-towered church, all mingle the present with the memory of many past years. The meeting at the little chapel was my first concern, and here a number of people from neighbouring hamlets had gathered.

I have two precious memories of my visit to Coxwold. First, I found myself staying in the lovely old house known as Shandy Hall. Its very date is wrapped in obscurity, and parts of it may well go back to the twelfth century. Here it was that Laurence Sterne lived and wrote, and it was from his famous book that the house was named. Here is the very room in which he penned his masterpiece, *Tristram Shandy,* and his other well known work, *A Sentimental Journey.* The old spot is much as it was when he knew it, odd and quaint in the extreme, and every part of the building alive and fascinating. The old rafters and beams that have held it together for hundreds of years, the floors, every one of which is on a different level from its neighbour, and also tilting unevenly in varied directions, all help to make the place charming. Sterne, it seems, was as quaint as the house in which he lived. We hear stories of how he spent his time fiddling and shooting, or writing humorous stories. Little wonder the villagers at Coxwold were perplexed and puzzled by him. But he made the whole world laugh. It was a great privilege to read some of his early work in the room where it was actually written, and to sleep in the room that had been his bedroom. I had been warned that there were ghosts in the house, but it was a delightful Tristram Shandy who kept me company that night—and some strange scratchings which ceased when I flung a book.

Near Coxwold is Newburgh Priory. This remarkable place, built on the site of an earlier monastery, some of the walls of which remain, is perhaps 800 years old. It came into private possession at the time of the Dissolution of the Monasteries, being given to the family of Belasyse. Recently Newburgh Priory has been turned into a successful public school, though it still belongs to its original owners. I called to see the headmaster and his wife, Mr. and Mrs. Daws. They were exceedingly kind. After coffee, I was shown over this place of treasures. Great works of art abound, and strange it was to walk round a school enriched with paintings by

Tintoretto, Hogarth, and scores of other famous artists. There is a massive marble fireplace from Venice, and everywhere art and refinement. The striking panelling and woodwork of this well preserved thirteenth-century priory astonished me; and when I think of the spacious park with its glorious lake, or of the beauty and charm of the house itself, I envy the boys who have the privilege of being taught there.

THE HEADLESS BENEFACTOR

But the outstanding interest, the unique possession which I had principally journeyed to see, was the tomb of Oliver Cromwell. The headless body of this benevolent dictator has been the object of much speculation, and also of much suspicion, but after hearing the story on the spot I felt strongly inclined to accept it. It appears that Cromwell's daughter brought the body of her father to this, her country home, and that it was buried in a stone tomb under the roof, the only approach to it being up a narrow flight of stairs. This, of course, was so that any attempts by Royalists could be beaten back. We know what happened to Cromwell's head after Charles II had his remains hung at Tyburn. This head is still in safe custody, but the tomb at Newburgh has never been opened, and it surely seems fit and proper that the two relics of Cromwell, the head and the body, should be brought together and honoured. Perhaps the day will come when this body at Newburgh will be rejoined to its head and reinterred in our National Abbey. This headless dictator possessed a head and a heart from which the dictators at present in the world could learn both wisdom and humanity. He deserves of our people the highest honour we can afford—even at this late date.

PART TWO

THE DALES

THE next morning Dick and I passed under the long bastion of the Hambleton Hills and near the village of Kilburn. High up on the hillside is a vast white horse. I was told that it was made originally by the village schoolmaster and some thirty men in 1857. This great horse can normally be seen for miles around, as can well be imagined when we learn that it is nearly 320 feet long and 228 feet high. On its big single eye it is possible for twenty people to sit. In peacetime this monster is constantly dressed in a thick coat of lime, but when I rode by the conspicuous landmark had been blackened over. Dick looked up more than once and then loudly sniffed with disdain at this creature, neither white nor black, but apparently trying to be both. Then he scampered off as though he could not tolerate such half-heartedness. But the tables were turned on him a few minutes later when we came upon a group of land girls who were waiting for a bus. They laughed. Dick, I am sure, would have said at me, though I will have it the other way. After a good laugh together these girls were intrigued when I suggested that I belonged to the same army as they. 'To what do you belong?' they asked.

'To the Church, which is like a mighty army', I explained, and then suggested that as the earth is the Lord's, for He made it, and He sustains it, therefore, all who work on the land must be in His army. The bronze faces of these girls smiled at the idea of changing jobs, though I am sure they understood that a parson must spend much time in ploughing and sowing in the human soil.

The next hundred miles or so took me into Wensleydale, and though we had meetings every day, the main interest was in the contacts made along the road. Let me share with you a few of the more amusing ones.

THE TEACHER TAUGHT

At one farm a young townsman who was on holiday asked if I would teach him to ride. It was fairly apparent from his timidity in approaching the horse that he would not quickly become proficient. 'What must I do?' he inquired.

'Only three things,' said I. 'The first thing is to learn to fall off.' We then spent a little time in learning how in an emergency it is wise to try and slip clear down the left shoulder of the horse.

'Next, you must learn to grip with your knees,' I went on. 'Few things are more necessary than to know how to use your knees. Lastly, you must keep a clear and steady head. These are the only three rules I know.'

I have a few genuine doubts about his ability to become a horseman, but judging from what he said, he knows how to ride something that is far more difficult. 'Come to think of it,' he said, 'life is like riding. One must know how to take a fall, for every man is thrown sometime, and it is wise to know how to take life's bumps. Certainly to use one's knees is a great necessity—most men fall because they use their knees so little! Neither would any one question the need for a clear, steady head.' I told him that he had given me a topic for my next meeting, and that I should not fail to use it. 'Well,' he said, 'I'm a local preacher. Is the copyright reserved?' I had never suspected it. It was but just retribution that a few days later my own deficiencies in horsemanship should be exposed.

DECLINE AND FALL

'Can you ride *anything*?' He stood there, surveying with the eye of an expert both my mount and myself. It was a curious greeting, for I had never met him before, and it was almost his first word. When I knew him better I found that this was characteristic of the way he always said as little as possible, and always went straight to the point. Another thing I later discovered was that he was not only a farmer, but a trainer of horses. At the time of which I write I knew nothing of this, and so, remembering my horse had carried me hundreds of miles, I said, 'I think so'.

A minute later I wished I had been more careful, for the farmer told me he had two young horses. He had just begun breaking them in the year before but had not been able to do anything with them during the winter. 'Would you like to try one?' he inquired.

Feeling that he was challenging me, I replied, 'Yes, by all means', though I did not say it very convincingly.

Early next morning we saddled the two-year-olds, and then, after several attempts, we got on their backs and started off down a lane. Never had I been on such a spirited mount. It was made of steel, it seemed, and was full of electricity. If only a leaf rustled in the hedge, or a piece of paper fluttered in the ditch, that alone was quite sufficient to set him jumping and scampering back. Eventually we came to a field where a clearing had been made around the outside of the wheat in preparation for the binder.

'Let's take them in here and give them a gallop,' my acquaintance suggested. It had already been as much as I could do to keep my saddle, but all I dare say was, 'Yes, certainly . . . er, of course'.

Away we galloped; and to my astonishment I was still on my horse's back after the first round.

'Well, they run all right together,' their owner said, 'but I guess they won't run apart. Suppose you take yours round, while I hold mine here.'

Off I went, while he struggled to hold his horse steady. I got about half-way round the field when *it* happened—and happened so quickly that I did not know it had happened until it was over. Suddenly, from the far side of the field, came a loud neigh. Immediately my horse became possessed with a desire for the heights. At any rate, his rear quarters leapt heavenwards while I, after an aerial circular tour, landed all square in the corn. It was a perfect throw.

I picked myself up with what little dignity remained and ran after my horse. Fortunately the reins were tangled round his fetlocks, so I caught him easily. I noticed, however, that I was in line of vision with my friend, so I struggled upon the horse's back, and trotted along. How I wish I could describe his face when we came alongside! It was a blank at first. Then it registered whimsical credulity. 'Did you come off?' he asked pointedly.

'Er . . . er . . . Yes. I don't think much of a horse that can't throw a man, do you?'

He was not impressed with this, so I went on to say, 'As a matter of fact, I came off when your horse neighed.'

'Aye,' he confessed, 'that's when I came off as well!'

Rarely have I been as grateful for anything as I was for this confession. We were great friends after that: and in passing let me add that I shall never listen to the song 'I hear you calling me' without remembering those two horses calling across the corn.

THE FLANK ATTACK

As a good piece of strategy it is often wise to appear to know less than one actually does—if possible. For instance: Seeing a boy following an implement up and down a field I waited until he came near the hedge and then called across, 'Good morning, what are you doing? Hoeing?'

He looked up, disdain on his face. How he pitied my ignorance! 'Hoeing! Nay, scruffling!' he jerked out.

'Well,' I called, 'you can see I know very little about farming. As a matter of fact, all I know is a very good story about scruffling. Would you like to hear it?'

Every countryman likes a good yarn, so I told him the story of the wheat and the tares, which, of course, I carefully called turnips and weeds. He listened without comment to this New Testament story in modern dress. It had linked his work with the Gospel, which was my main purpose, and I think he pondered it as he went up and down the fields.

This method (which might be called a flank attack) was employed when I encountered a man cleaning out ditches by the roadside. Looking at him brought back to my mind the familiar word about *Make this valley full of ditches.* I asked him what would happen if the ditches were not cleaned out.

'Why,' he replied, looking surprised at so simple a question, 'you would soon have the land swampy and useless.'

Timidly I asked, for I was not sure of my man, if he did not think that the trouble with the world was that the ditches had not been cleaned out. Seeing he was interested and intrigued we went on to think together of the morass into which the world has fallen, and how we needed new drainage systems. He agreed even when I went on to suggest that in the new world-order, of which we were hearing so much, we badly needed the old ditches cleaned and new ones dug. Still hesitantly, I shot my last arrow and suggested that even this would not be enough unless we had the streams of God's grace flowing through them. 'Empty ditches are unhealthy,' I added.

'Look here,' he burst out, 'I'm a Methodist. I wonder if you'd mind if I share this line of thought with my class of boys down at the chapel?'

After that we got along finely.

This way of finding openings by asking questions led me to a remarkable open gate, literally as well as metaphorically. It happened like this:

Jim was kneeling on the ground hammering away at a broken gate he had unhinged. By way of greeting I said that it was good to find a spot without a gate. 'I seem to have spent most of the last two or three weeks opening and shutting gates,' I told him.

'But wouldn't a farm be in a poor way without them?' was his response.

'Why?' I asked.

Jim was not quite sure whether I was ignorant or simply teasing, so with slight irritation he said: 'Do you want all the beasts to wander off where they like, spoiling the crops and fighting with each other?'

'No,' I said, 'but they are doing it already, you know.'

His eye lit up with a twinkle, and I knew he would enjoy a yarn, so I attempted to explain how much of the world's trouble to-day is because the gates are down, and many of the beasts have escaped to destroy and fight. There were commandments in life, I reminded him, like the well-known Ten which must be obeyed. 'Some people', I went on, 'only remember the commandment, *Don't be found out*; and also, *Go where you like* and, *Do what you like*. Don't you think that the gates of law and love are both essential, for life will only work one way, and that's God's way?'

'Well,' he drawled slowly, 'I've mended scores of gates in my time, but I never thought of it that way before.'

As I scrambled back into the saddle, I called out, 'Do you know the gate that leads to the little chapel down the street?'

'Aye, it used to be an iron one,' he answered, 'but they have a small wooden one now.'

'Yes, that's so,' I agreed. 'Don't forget to use it!'

BY THE POND

That evening, after supper, I took a walk down to the main street of the village where I was staying and eventually sat down on a rough seat near a pond. Village . . . England . . . peace, and a quiet splendour! Behind me a few old elms rustled sleepily. From the cottage windows lamplight shone, for it was not yet blackout time. Far down the valley other lights were showing faintly from scattered farms and an occasional hamlet. I watched the pointed pines on the edge of the moors sway solemnly in the evening wind. Quietude . . . serenity . . . content. As the silence seeped into my spirit I reflected that many people would find health if only they could value and use the country aright. This was worth more than all the mob adulation received by dictators. Surely in such a place men could not be other than content. Pondering in this way I noticed a man coming nearer. From his stooping gait and air of dejection I could tell something was wrong. My judgement was that he would be about fifty-five though the gathering gloom made it difficult to discern details very clearly. This man shattered many of my dreams about the contentment of the countryman, for he was contemplating taking his own life. He was quite determined about it; and, to my great astonishment, was almost anxious to discuss it.

'I'm finished', he told me decisively after a few minutes' conversation. 'I've had quite enough of it.' He seemed to age as he spoke.

'Already?'

'Of the sort of life I've had, yes.'

'Of the sort it *has been*, you mean?'

'Do you mean the rest might be different?' he demanded.

'I mean the rest might be better, more worth while.'

'Better!' Nothing can convey the scorn of that single outburst.

For a moment I was helpless. Presently, however, I began again. 'Look,' I said, 'you see those houses and farms with the lights twinkling? Don't they mean anything to you?'

'No, they don't mean a thing.'

'Well, I don't know the people in the houses, but I have learned to love folk and these places mean a lot to me.'

'They've no meaning for me,' he declared. 'I know what you mean though. Here we are, you and I, looking at the same things at the same moment, from, as nearly as possible, the same position. You see something significant, I see nothing. It's the old story about a man's personal view of a thing that matters, isn't it? What we individually make of it, eh? That's what you were going to say, isn't it?' His thin lips curled in derision. 'Just like a ruddy parson! You're the chap who has been preaching over there this evening, aren't you?'

'I am,' I agreed. 'It's what you should expect from a parson.'

And that, I imagined, would be the end of it. He seemed too bitter to listen.

But suddenly he sat down beside me and took another line.

'I'm doing it', he said, 'because I have no faith left. *Just that.*'

'By the way, you're not a countryman?' I asked.

'Yes, though I was once a school teacher in a city.'

We sat there with the breeze rustling through the trees. Neither spoke for a long time.

'*The spirit bloweth where it listeth.* Do you know who said that?'

'Yes, I know. I know more than you suspect I know,' he said quietly.

'Then, although we are both sitting at the same spot and looking at the same things we do now see something alike?—You see this path around the pond! Let's walk around.'

As we went I took his arm and said, 'You told me you had lost your faith. Of course you haven't. You've only lost your faith in life, but faith always works in two directions. You still have faith in death. You believe that is a way out—perhaps into a void, but a way out. You *believe* that. See! We have walked in a circle around this pond (here we sat down again) and returned to the same spot. Your thinking has been going round in circles too. But remember there is another way of getting out of the circle besides jumping into the pond: you could strike out on a new path. You could take that path to the right—which, by the way, leads up to the chapel. Get me?' He did.

The rest was personal, and I will only say he is still alive.

RHABDOMANCING

After leaving the Wensleydale area and spending some little time in the old cathedral city of Ripon, Dick and I jogged along to a small village named Burton Leonard. The two lovely old greens at this place were bright in the sunshine, and it was easy, by giving a few children rides on Dick, to collect them for a meeting. Indeed, many of these stayed to the adult meeting which followed. Though this meeting was not so large as many, it was good to see a number of keen young cyclists who had come from as far afield as Ripon and Harrogate.

After these gatherings I had one of the thrills of my life, for my host, a fine Rhabdomancer, whose sparkling eyes revealed a merry heart, endeavoured to introduce me to the art of water-divining.

From a nearby hedge he cut a V-shaped hazel twig. Holding an end of this in each hand, he began walking about the field. Soon he came to a spot where the twig began to twist, rising in a most surprising way until it stood up vertically.

I was all eagerness to do what he had done: so, taking the twig in my hand I tried to follow his example. But I might as well have been in the waterless Sahara for all the effect it had. Try as I would, nothing happened, and my enthusiasm sank to zero.

'You see,' he explained, 'you either have it, or you haven't.' Then he tried to console me by saying that water-divining is the art of the illiterate. This might have impressed me if he himself had not been so intelligent and so well educated. In my heart I knew he meant one was either in harmony with the nature of things or not. Nevertheless, I had learned my first lesson. One either has it or is without; and surely that is also true of genuine religion. There can be no doubt, no half-measures.

Again I turned to him and said, 'Look here, if I haven't it, how can I get it?'

Seeing that I was really interested, he promised to show me; and so, while he took one end of the twig in his right hand, I took the other in my left. Then we held each other by the hand and walked towards the spot where, deep down, we knew there was running water. To my intense satisfaction we no sooner drew near to the spot than the twig began to twist upward until it finally stood erect, rather like a 'V' for Victory.

I had learned my second lesson. If one has not got it, the method of getting it is to link oneself to some one who has. Surely, that too was true of real religion? It is always caught from some one else, rather than learned as a theory, especially, of course, by linking oneself to the Supreme Diviner, one who discovers the waters of life in the most barren places. Suddenly I remembered something, so I said, 'But I shall not always be with you. How shall I manage then?'

He smiled, and said, 'You and I are very different; perhaps it would work if you tried with a bigger twig, and began where there is more water.'

All the following morning as Dick trotted along the road I was thinking of this, and that perhaps I needed a bigger twig and more water. When, a little later, we came in sight of the River Ouse, with its broad sweeping current, I laughed aloud at the thought which whispered that I should try here. Nothing venture, nothing win; so I tied up my horse, and from a hedge cut a fairly large twig at least twice the size of the first we had used. There and then I started walking towards the bridge. I held the twig before me. Intently I watched it. Did it move, or was it imagination? But, oh joy, when I was nearing the bridge the rapture of the discoverer flooded me, for the twig moved!

All this time I had been so absorbed in my experiment that only casually had I noticed a number of folk looking on. I was sure by their smiles that many thought me queer. A few gathered round to find out what I was doing. Others joined them. These were the first, though I am certain others will have to hear the message of the Divining Rod. It clearly says three things. You either have it, or you have not. If you have not you may get it by linking yourself to some one who has. Maybe the reason why it is not working in your case is because you are trying with a little instead of a lot. Many would find religion work if they had a bigger Christ, if they left the shallows and tried the deeps.

THE CONCEITED COUNSELLOR

The next twenty miles were to take us to Marston Moor, and the country roads afforded not only good riding but good hunting. There were, for instance, parties of soldiers tending the searchlights, and groups of folk waiting for buses. All these supplied opportunities for contacts. Furthermore, in this district I was hard on the heels of John Wesley. At Staveley, for instance, I was able to stand on a tombstone, close by the church door, that he had used as a pulpit.

Then there were the labourers building a haystack. They gave me a laugh which lasted a long time. Something prompted me to speak to these men, and I have always found it wise to respond to such promptings lest one become less responsive. So I urged Dick to canter across the field, and, knowing that a Yorkshireman hates conceit as much as deceit, I made a few commonplace remarks, and then rudely added:

'If I were building that stack I'd do it very differently.'

They looked at me as if I were a puppy. Then one asked gruffly, 'How would *you* do it?'

I confessed that I'd build it in such a way that it would fall down in two days. They saw the joke and joined in the laugh, and mutual confidence was not only restored but cemented.

'By the way,' I told them. 'I know nothing about building a stack, but why need you take so much care?'

One of them explained that it must be built closely enough so that it would not let in the rain, and would also withstand the storms. He gave some graphic instances of how in a great wind the previous April many stacks had been swept away. This gave me a fine opportunity of inventing a story about a man who built a stack, without considering either where or how it was built—a man who found that when the storms came and the floods descended, it was swept away. It was only right at the end that they realized that I had been preaching a sermon about building the house of life on sound principles.

'Bust it, chaps,' said one, 'this'll be that riding parson I've heard of!'

'Maybe,' I replied, 'but would you agree that Life can only be built one way if it is not to bust, and that *that* is God's way? Cheerio!'

BULLETS

Approaching the village of Long Marston the first thing I encountered was a newly built obelisk marking the site of the famous battle of Marston Moor on July 6, 1644. It stands at the edge of a track called 'Bloody Lane' where so much of the carnage took place. Ever since I had had to study the details of this battle at school I had longed to visit the site; and I was determined, therefore, to make the most of this first visit. Quickly I rode to the top of the hill known as the Clump because of the cluster of trees still to be found there. It was here that Cromwell, sitting astride his horse, had directed the course of the battle; and it was around this hillside that he had swung in his decisive attack to the discomfiture of Prince Rupert. From this vantage spot it was, and still is, possible to observe the battlefield.

At the foot of this hill live a splendid Methodist family with whom it was a privilege to stay. Mr. Abbey, whose ancestor had fought in the battle, told me how his forebears had lived on this site right down the years, and how, even yet, he ploughs up bullets and weapons that were used in the battle.

Sitting by the monument, I wished it had not been so far from the village so that a meeting might have been arranged on this historic spot. However, I was joined by a Royal Air Force boy, and we began discussing the battle. He was a keen student of the past, and it was impossible not to feel that in the Royal Air Force we have a modern counterpart of Cromwell's Ironsides. This young pilot was handling horsepower very different from, and much greater than, that known by Cromwell's riders.

'Do you think the battle was won right here?'

'No, I'm certain it was not,' I replied. 'I think it was won at Knaresborough.'

'Knaresborough! Why, that's eight miles away!'

This fine boy was keenly interested in the story of how Cromwell, on the night before the battle, rode back to Knaresborough Castle. There, it seems, he was lost. His men searched the castle high and low, till at last, with the aid of a little serving-maid, he was found in a small disused room at the top of the castle. He was on his knees, an open Bible before him. For two hours he had been seeking and praying for guidance. No wonder that Cromwell routed his foes next day, for he tells us that he felt sure he was in line with the Divine will, and that during the battle he was carried along by a Divine compulsion.

'Don't you think,' I asked, 'that what a man *does* in public is determined by what he *is* in private, and that in that little room at Knaresborough the battle was really won?' My modern Ironside agreed that Cromwell's open Bible and prayer were symbolic of what we need to-day, though he said with a lovely frankness that his practice did not warrant his agreement, for he did not pray much.

This roguish-faced boy was the type for whom one would readily do anything; he was so sincere. We talked of the principles of flying, and of how in the final analysis it is nothing inside but something outside a plane that makes it rise. It may have good and powerful engines, and a technically perfect 'set' to its wings, but all these merely co-operate with an outside power which gives the lift. So man cannot lift himself. He depends on linking up with a power outside himself. When, finally, I suggested that he had a good strong body (a fine engine), and a good, keen, clean mind (a splendid 'set' to his wings), and that all he needed was a power outside himself, and that prayer was the means of linking oneself to such power, he said quietly:

'My father was a Christian and used to talk like that—*you're shooting his bullets.*'

I hope that there on that battlefield of Marston Moor a father's bullet found its mark.

AT THE PALACE

After spending Sunday in York, Dick and I struck out on Monday morning from Marston in the direction of Selby. The route lay through Bishopthorpe, and so, recalling the kindly interest of the Archbishop of York, Dr. Garbett, and how he had invited me to call should I ever be passing, I rode up to the old palace where for centuries the Primates of the English Church have been housed. The Archbishop was not at home (having gone upon a walking tour among his people) but Dick was left grazing on the Palace lawn while the Archbishop's secretary kindly entertained me. I was examining the famous old dining-room when the secretary ran in exclaiming: 'Your horse has gone, Mr. Newman!'

'Gone?'

'Yes, he's nowhere in sight!'

We hurried to the front of the Palace. As I rushed through the gateway I hailed a passing cyclist. 'Have you seen anything of a black horse?' I asked.

'Yes, you'll find him round the corner,' he told me.

Turning the corner, I saw an amusing scene. There stood Dick by the garage, critically surveying the Archbishop's car, while the smiling chauffeur, an ex-cavalryman, was looking on.

'The old and the new,' he commented.

I recalled how Dr. Garbett had humorously told me once that a bishop's gaiters and the cords around his hat and sleeves were all relics of the days when such dignitaries rode on horseback round their dioceses. 'I'm always dressed for riding,' he said.

I am certain by the contemptuous expression on Dick's face that he was regarding this car as a usurper, and comforting himself with the reflection that the conservatism which leads a bishop to retain his riding habit is a high tribute to the Church's love of horses. 'You are only tolerated' he seemed to be saying to the car.

As I stood on the old mounting block from which so many dignitaries had mounted their horses, my heart was full of thankfulness, for I thought of the new mutuality and brotherhood now uniting members of the varied churches. The intolerance of a past age is going: and then came to mind that strange little incident which has trickled down to us from the eighteenth century about two men, equally great: Bishop Butler and John Wesley. Wesley, who was travelling in the Bishop's diocese, called to ask his advice; and the following conversation took place:

Bishop: 'Well, sir, since you ask my advice I will give it freely. You have no business here; you are not commissioned to preach in this diocese. Therefore I advise you to go hence.'

Wesley: 'My lord, my business on earth is to do what good I can. Wherever, therefore, I think I can do most good, there I must stay as long as I think fit. At present I think I do most good here therefore here I stay.'

These two sons of Oxford parted company abruptly at that point, and never met again. I cannot think that such intolerance reflected credit on either. How vastly better and bigger is the present eagerness for co-operation and mutual appreciation.

THE FERRY

It was the Archbishop's chauffeur who told me of the ferry. At this point the river is both broad and deep, and there are no bridges nearer than York. To hear of this ferry was indeed good fortune, for it would save miles of riding and hours of time. Soon after leaving Bishopthorpe, therefore, we travelled along the river bank until we reached a place where a large piece of metal hung. By violently hammering on this one attracts the attention of the ferryman on the other side. Rapidly he came across in his small, flat craft, which, after some persuasion, we managed to get Dick to trust.

'It's a long time,' said the ferryman, 'since I had to take a horse over.' Then after a pause he said, 'But I know who *you* are. You're the Methodist preacher, and you are going to Riccall.' Apparently he was a reader of the daily press.

'By the way,' I said, 'did Wesley ever come across by this ferry?'

'No, he would have come across down there', said the ferryman as he pointed to a spot half a mile down the river. It was there 172 years before that Wesley himself had been ferried across. Such memories still persist.

It was a good thing that so much time had been gained, for the day was to be crowded with adventure. After passing through Naburn and Stillingfleet, we cut away from the main roads, taking lanes through ripening corn fields. At almost every turn of the road there seemed to be some one of interest to whom to speak, but perhaps the most fascinating was an old man who asked me what I thought of Mussolini's downfall—the news had been given that morning. He was intrigued when I told him that years ago I had seen that creature in Rome, and had heard him shouting about the glorious Italian army in Abyssinia. The old man put down his hedge-hook, clearly expecting me to say more.

'May I tell you how the whole thing appears to me?' I began. 'I've always felt that Mussolini was saying, "I can do just as I like; no one, not even God, can stop me. I attack helpless Albania, even on Good Friday, and God does nothing. I mow down the Abyssinians with gas when they fight too well with ordinary weapons, and God cannot stop me. When France is weak I stab her in the back, and my successes continue." 'He forgot', I went on, 'that the Psalmist says wickedness may flourish for a season but is soon cut down. Our grandfathers saw how this worked out in the case of Napoleon; the early Christians say how it worked out in the case of Nero; and we have seen it work out against Mussolini. History is really God's story. It is not a heap of stones, but a mosaic. These men forget that God fits even the black stones into the design of His purpose.'

I had been so carried away on one of my favourite themes that I had not noticed how long I had been talking.

'That's funny,' he broke in. 'I don't know who you are, but that's the way our old vicar talks.'

Without meaning to be egotistic I replied, 'Then your old vicar is right, and if I lived here I'd go and hear such a man next Sunday. Will you?'

He screwed up his face, and then slowly and deliberately said, 'I will'.

DEAD DANES AND LIVING ITALIANS

For long years I had wanted to visit Riccall for I knew that this was the place where, in 1066, a fleet of Norsemen had invaded England. Who has not been thrilled with the story of how our king Harold offered his renegade relative a third of the kingdom if he would make peace? 'And what will you give Tostig, the Dane?' was the proud reply.

'Six feet of good English soil,' said Harold boldly.

A few days later, in the battle of Stamford Bridge, six feet of earth was all Tostig received. The invaders were decisively beaten, and out of the three hundred ships that came to Riccall, only twenty-four sailed away.

The spot where this abortive attempt at invasion was made is about two miles from the village. Never expecting to see the result of a more recently attempted invasion, I rode along to the place, and there, thanks to a farmer who owns the fields along the banks of this historic river, still flowing strong and deep through the land of the free, I was able to satisfy my curiosity about the past. Incidentally, the farmer told me how, in 1912, when digging deeply in his fields, he came across a number of skulls and relics which experts confirmed had belonged to the Danes; these have since found their way into our national museums. The interest of this old story, however, was eclipsed for me in a most remarkable way.

Curiously enough, quite near to this spot, we met a group of people who in our day had thought of invading England. About a dozen Italian prisoners of war stood by the roadside awaiting collection by lorry. At many points on the road I had talked to such men, but rarely with better results than now. Having attempted a little Italian, only to find it was so bad that they understood my English better, I was relieved to find that one knew German. Together we managed to speak to the others. And what a small world this is! How strange that this man who came from Naples should know fairly intimately an Italian friend of mine who used to live some six miles from that city! The Italians were delighted that anyone should speak to them, and we chatted happily for some time. Then I asked them what they thought of English people.

'Some good, some bad', said the boldest of them cautiously, and then proceeded to give me instances of both kinds.

'There is no doubt you are right,' I agreed. 'But the British prisoners in Italy will be saying just the same about the Italians, some good, some bad.'

They nodded agreement.

'Isn't our real task just this,' I asked, 'to make bad Englishmen into good Englishmen and bad Italians into good Italians?'

Yes, they thought it was.

'Then how can we do it?' Here I drew a blank, for they did not know.

When I pulled out of my pocket a small German Testament and quoted a word from the Master which, I thought, met the case, they looked astonished beyond words, and crossing themselves asked if I were a priest.

'No, not a priest, but some one who is trying to tell everywhere of One who said any one could be free, even though forced to live as prisoners.' The short prayer, given in a language they did not know, would lose nothing because of that, I fancy.

Then, up came their lorry. Each pressed my hand warmly, and some expressed the hope that we should meet when they were free.

THE PUBLICAN

Arriving at the village green in Riccall I met a traveller who explained that the owners of the local inn were no longer able, under war conditions, to provide meals. However, I went along and asked if I might house Dick in the stable. The publican's wife, a kindly soul, not only offered me the use of the stable, but insisted on my sharing a meal. She obviously knew all about my purpose in the village, for she quickly said, with a smile, 'You must not think that we are heathens because we keep a public-house. My husband was brought up a Wesleyan, I'm a churchwoman.' This hit me harder than she knew, for my own attitude to the drink trade is one of uncompromising hostility, and only the previous day I had been attacking it vigorously. However, this woman and her husband were most kind, and not only refused payment, but offered me the shelter of their home whenever I needed it. I can only say that I think theirs is the kind of inn where the Master would have been at home.

The meetings which followed were greatly helped by a splendid company of young folk who cycled out from Selby. First, we had a service in the church; later we marched, singing joyously, through the streets in a procession to the green. Then followed an open-air meeting under the trees. It was shared by the local vicar; and finally came the happy and inevitable talks to the children. It had been a glorious day. Starting from the battlefield at Marston; pausing at midday in an Archbishop's Palace; on through the scenes of pastoral peace to the place of invasion; tea in a public-house, and (I must not forget to mention) half an hour spent in a gipsy encampment by the road; all this and four meetings in one day! Could anyone desire greater opportunities?

The next few days provided some excellent riding over the flat but varied valleys of the Ouse and Derwent. It would be possible to tell at length of the visit to Pocklington, with its lovely old grammar school where William Wilberforce was a scholar, or of the service held in the square of that old market town. At even greater length one might write of the stay in a village, as lovely as its name, Barton-le-Willows, where it was their Anniversary. There, in ways typical of Yorkshire Methodism, the folk did full justice both to the meetings and the meals. All this, however, I pass over in order to make haste towards one of the most remarkable experiences of the pilgrimage.

HEARTS ARE TRUMPS

It came about like this: After several hours' riding up and down among lovely, wooded hills, we eventually came again to the Derwent valley just above the glorious old ruins of Kirkham Priory. It is interesting to note that this fascinating place was built in memory of a boy who was thrown from his horse and killed. The spot is still marked by the remains of an old stone cross just in front of the Abbey gateway.

Riding among the trees on the hill I approached the beautiful old bridge which leads to the Priory. At the entrance to the bridge was a notice saying, 'Bridge Demolished'. After carefully examining the structure under the watchful eyes of soldiers, Dick and I failed to find anything wrong. So, cautiously, we went across. Once at the other side more soldiers came up. These questioned me suspiciously. Still, we were allowed to pass. A little farther on it was possible to see in the distance tanks charging across the fields, and to hear the rattle of their guns. Even after noticing a number of soldiers, their guns at the ready as they crept cautiously around the hedgerows, the truth failed to dawn on me, and into the valley of death I rode.

Sitting by the side of a wood I noticed a small group of soldiers. With a cheery 'Good day', I stopped for my customary word, when to my bewilderment, one said in a deep sepulchral voice, 'Sorry, we're dead!'

'Dead?'

'Yes,' said another, grinning, 'I'm the fellow that's burying 'em.'

Then the meaning of the demolished bridge and the questioning soldiers became clear. I was in the midst of a vast battlefield.

'What's it like to be dead?' I bantered.

'Not too bad', said a most attractive corpse, looking up from a game of cards three of them were playing. This man was playing a spare hand for his pal, who, apparently, was still living.

'Suppose I died for fifteen minutes, would you mind if I took that "dummy" hand?' I queried.

They moved around to make room, and I tied up Dick near some lush, paradisial grass (he thought it was heavenly, I think) and sat down among the 'dead'.

'How shall we play?' inquired one of the 'deceased'.

'Well, I know a topping new way to play whist,' I assured him. 'It takes just five hands. Would you like me to show you?'

First we played 'no trumps', and while doing so I tried to point out how a pack of cards is supposed to symbolize life—many play 'no trumps', every man for himself. Nothing has more value than anything else, and everything must serve one's own ends. *Get what you can, how you can, for yourself*, that is the policy of 'no trumps' I reminded them. For our next hand we had clubs as trumps. It was easy to show how some think that clubs always win. 'Clubs are a relic of jungle days when one sought to batter down opponents by force,' I went on. 'The dictators have used this old method. Why, you fellows have been killed by clubs! I suppose clubs have their place in the game of life, as when the policeman uses his truncheon. But clubs prove who is strongest, not who is right.'

The soldiers beat me at clubs. We then turned to diamonds. How many think diamonds is life's best hand! Wealth is their pursuit. 'Of course,' I said, 'it may win sometimes, but so often it resorts to nasty tricks, any one can demonstrate the trickery of wealth.' Spades gave me the chance of saying how some people believed that if one only digs and works hard enough, life will satisfy. Spades is, of course, very much better than spoofing with diamonds or biffing with clubs, but it is not life's trump hand. 'Not the labours of my hands and not the powers of the mind can satisfy my life,' I said. 'There is a mysterious something bigger than both.'

Hearts gave me the chance I had wanted, and by sheer good fortune (or was it something more?) I had a good hand. If only men's hearts were right, what a glorious world!

'He's got us *this* time,' one remarked, as I kept bringing out heart after heart from my hand; yet deliberately keeping back the ace. 'One day, you know,' I told them, 'when you and I are really dead, it's hearts that will win, and we shall find that God holds the Master trump.'

Down went my ace.

'He both is and has the Ace of Hearts,' I concluded.

Most of this conversation had been given with smiles and humour, but those 'dead' men had listened. In the midst of death we had pondered the game of life, and I rather fancy that those men will never play whist again without remembering this interpretation of it.

It was truly funny when one said, 'Well, I don't know who you are, but you ought to be a parson.'

Having leapt into the saddle I left them by saying, 'Cheerio, boys, I'm something of a padre, and I hope to meet you all at the resurrection.'

Never, I think, have I played a more profitable game.

THE VILLAGE GREEN

I have often referred to a meeting on a village green, and before leaving the moors and dales it might be well to give one typical picture of a village meeting. There were between forty and fifty such, but I select the one at Slingsby, for from here we journey naturally to the Wolds.

When we were still some eight miles from the village, I knew something was going to happen, for a passing cyclist greeted me with the words, 'I know where *you* are going!'

'Oh, where?'

'Slingsby, and they are expecting you!'

This led me to guess that publicity agents had been at work. It became clearer when, entering the village, several mothers came out and called to their children, saying, 'Eh, cum here and look at the preacher'.

It was abundantly clear when, coming to the green, I saw that some one had brought out a number of chairs and forms and that not only was every seat occupied, but a large number of people stood around under the trees. Nothing had been forgotten. There was a piano, and even a groom to take charge of Dick.

We were just going to begin the meeting when the local rector walked up. He readily responded to an invitation to lead us in prayer. 'May God bless this meeting', he said simply and earnestly, and if ever a prayer was answered this surely was. To borrow appropriate language from Wesley's journal: 'For an hour the people listened without movement.' Incidentally, Wesley himself had preached on this green. Noting the piano, I recalled that in the hymn-book there is a tune called 'Slingsby', and I asked if they could sing it. Sing it? They could! They sang with a fervour and harmony that might have been envied by many a city choir. I shall never sing that tune again without seeing the cheerful crowd singing it in the village after which it is named. Later, I discovered that the tune had been written by the son of a predecessor of the vicar present with us.

What were the results of such meetings?

I can only tell the facts. After one such meeting a woman, whose newly lit eyes were in striking contrast to some new deep lines on her face, came up to say how, a few days before, she had heard the tragic news that her son had been killed in the Middle East. She had contemplated taking her own life, for there seemed to be nothing left worth having. But in the meeting she found a new hope and a new light, and she had taken a new grip on life.

Three months after the meeting described above I was sitting one Saturday night in my Scarborough home when a knock came at the door. There I found a young farmer. He began by telling me that he did not expect I should know him, and that he had been at the meeting on the green at Slingsby.

'Since then,' he said, 'I've been very unhappy, and at long last I've come to see you.' Notice that he had travelled thirty miles three months afterwards to ask this simple but vital question: 'Can I get what you that night said any man could have? Nothing else will meet my need.' There, in my room, two of us quietly gave our lives to God.

Many such records could be given, but I feel that they are so utterly personal and private that they should be written in the Book of Life rather than in this one.

PART THREE

THE WOLDS

So we leave the villages of the plains for the Wolds—the nearest thing in England to Canadian prairies. Sweeping miles of undulating fertile country, they have patches of green, gold, and brown all intermixed, and occasionally enlivened by splashes of crimson poppies. To sit on a Wold top and watch the wind play among the corn is like seeing a vast sea of colour in fascinating motion.

Little villages are hidden away in the most unexpected places among these sweeping highlands. Often they are quite invisible until one comes to the last tip that leads down to them.

One such is a little hamlet known as Kirby-Grindalythe. Here I had the joy of sharing in the reopening of a little chapel which had been closed for fourteen years. Just prior to my arrival a Methodist family had come to live there—seven children and their parents. They not only felt pain at seeing this little sanctuary closed, but started to pray and work for its opening. They had already cleaned and painted it before I saw it. We had an afternoon meeting, and the fact that there were but five people did not inspire great hope. However, at night the little place was packed to capacity. At the children's service gathered 29 out of the 33 children in the village. It is most gratifying to record that as the result of this devoted family's work, and the reopening of the church, every Sunday sees a fine congregation assembling, and a Sunday school of 25 young people. How much our villages owe to such families. One such can remake a whole village—given only that they harness work to their prayer, and sincerity to both.

AT THE CROSS-ROADS

He was sitting by the cross-roads when I first met him. Then he had been dressed in shirt and shorts and was evidently hiking.

'Can you tell me where I am?' were his first words.

'No. Are you lost?'

'Yes, there is an old sign lying here under the hedge on which names can faintly be seen, but it's not much use for I don't know which finger points where. Do you know where these five roads lead?'

Remembering a story I had once heard I ignored his question and asked, 'But where have you come from?'

'Well, I started out from Pocklington but I've been cutting across country and lost my bearings: it's not where I came from that matters but where I want to be.'

'Forgive me,' I said, 'but it makes *all* the difference. If a fellow knows where he came from, it is often easy to see the way forward. I'm as uncertain of my way as you, but because I know where I came from I can set up that post with its finger pointing back to something I know and the way forward is clear.'

His eyes sparkled hopefully. 'Ah, now, where have you come from?'

'God. We all have.'

'Where?'

'God.'

'You mean . . .'

'I mean that when a man is lost, if he can look back to a fine home or a good church or to some definite Christian certainty, that past in his life is likely to show him the way forward.'

A delightful ten minutes followed in which we talked about those who, by taking short cuts and cross cuts in life, also cut themselves off from the best things in life's background. Then we raised up the old signpost, took our bearings, exchanged addresses, and shook hands. He took the high road and I took the by-road.

Recently he called to see me. This time he was dressed in the uniform of an army officer.

THE SWING OF A SCYTHE

It was not far from these cross-roads that I made five fine new friends. When I first met them they were making a clearing in a cornfield preparatory to the binder starting its work. For a time I watched them swinging their scythes. Then I rode up to the gate.

'Is it hard to swing a scythe?' I inquired.

I noticed that one winked at the others and they all grinned. So I continued, 'I always like having a go once at anything. Do you mind if I try?'

As they were more than delighted, I picked up a scythe and began to swing it. Swinging a scythe is not nearly so simple as it looks. The men, I noticed, had moved to safe distances from me, and soon they chuckled hugely at my efforts. So, explaining that though I knew very little about farming, yet I did know a few good farming stories, and as it was nearly their lunch time, I wondered if they would like to hear them during lunch. While they ate I told them, of course in modern language and with slight variations, the story of the Good Sower and the harvest he had hoped to reap. My dissimulation must have been bad, for they soon discovered that I was a parson, but did not seem to like me the less for that. When we parted we shook hands like old friends, and I sincerely hope and expect that another harvest than that reaped by the scythes will come out of that field.

A SPIRITED GALLOP

Thanks to these men I found my way to an old Roman road which was to save me many miles. This old road, over which I knew Wesley had travelled many times on his way to Pocklington, consists of a wide grassy surface, and runs for several miles between high hedges. It is very little used to-day. Perhaps a psychic expert could explain what happened there. I cannot. All I know is that something took possession of Dick's mind. Whether it was the spirit of Black Bess calling him, or one of Wesley's horses still on the road, or whether he saw some of the old Roman chariots still rushing on their way, I know not. What I do know is that he took to his heels and galloped as I had never known him gallop before. Nothing, it seemed, could stop him. After many attempts I contented myself with the reflection that if *he* could keep going I certainly could, and that he would tire first. The whole scene must have looked strange. My haversack was bobbing up and down on my back, while my hair was streaming in the breeze. Men in the fields looked on astonished, thinking perhaps that John Gilpin was off to town again.

At length the road came abruptly to an end, terminating on a wide, modern macadam road. Dick stopped as abruptly as he had started, and when he turned his head from this new road and looked round at me, there was such complete contempt in his expression that I shall for ever know what horses think of our boasted modern roads. He would have scampered back.

Just at the point where we stopped, a countryman was at work. He almost gaped at my panting horse while he said, 'My word, he's got a fine spirit'.

'Spirit?' By this time I was always on the look-out for an opening, and 'spirit' was a religious word. The door was open for a conversation on the difference a good or bad spirit can make to life.

At the end of another gallop two days later I did not get things all my own way. We had stopped by a house where a decorator was at work. 'What do you think you are doing?' was the unfriendly greeting he gave. 'Do you think you are imitating that young parson chap?'

'Parson chap! What do you mean?'

Then he told me a few things about a riding parson who had been in his village a few nights before, and I heard a few things about myself that I would rather not pass on.

Ignoring his comments, I asked if when painting he came to a piece of rotten wood, he would paint over it or cut it out.

'Why, cut it out, of course,' he growled.

'Don't you think that one of the troubles with most of us', I asked 'is that instead of cutting the rotten out of our lives we try to gloss it over? Much of the trouble with the world to-day is that while on the outside it looks all right, underneath it's rotten.'

By this time a man who knew me had joined us. He looked up at the decorator and said: 'Don't you know who this is?' Then he told him.

RIDING AND RHYTHM

There is one of these Wold villages that I shall always remember. Many things combine to give it a permanent niche in my mind—the remarkable meeting presided over by a local canon, the man who afterwards told us he had clearly seen the light, and that, God helping him, he would follow it, and especially the unusual character who proposed a vote of thanks.

He started by telling us that years ago an old lay preacher used to travel regularly to that village on horseback. Yet, although this man knew a lot about horses and brought a good horse, he always had a saddle that would not fit. We were all puzzled as to what he meant by a saddle that would not fit, and like a practised deceiver he kept repeating the phrase. At length he explained that this preacher always had a good sermon but a text that wouldn't fit it. 'The text,' he said, 'was his own, but the sermon was usually one of Talmage's. Many a Sunday night before he started home we would harness up his horse with the right saddle.' What a lovely way to condemn plagiarism! This foolish preacher had imagined that out in a village he had less intelligent people in his congregation, and that they would not know if a thing were his own or not. After touring scores of these villages I am convinced that it is not possible to distinguish between the intellectual standard of town and country. In many village chapels sit those who have a university training and who read wisely and well.

How strange it was that the next day the man who told us this amusing yarn should have had the tables turned on him. He had said that he would like to ride along with me although he had not ridden a horse for twenty-five years. So he borrowed a splendid little white pony from the farm at which I was saying, and we set off together. I had offered him the use of Dick, but seeing that my steed was over sixteen hands he declined in favour of the smaller, saying that there would be less distance to fall. What followed was really comical. Dick takes long, sweeping strides, but the little pony took short snappy steps. Both Dick and the pony insisted on trotting, and my friend with his legs outstretched, was going up and down like a shuttlecock. When we finally stopped, after some eight miles, his face was a picture. He could not get off; and when at length he *did*, he could not stand. When he tried to walk, he waddled. He had, it seemed, completely forgotten how to ride. Three days later I saw him emerging from a shop in his village—he still hobbled. Coming up, he said, 'I've a bill for you, for so many bandages, so much embrocation, and yards of new skin that I shall have to grow.'

I mention that incident for this reason: *Riding is an art.* It involves moving with rhythm and poise. The effects on the mind caused by riding a horse and that caused by driving a mechanical vehicle are as different as can be imagined. Most of us are drivers —the early preachers were riders. I am certain this has a profound effect both on the way our minds work and on the messages created. For instance, it is common knowledge that many of Charles Wesley's poems came to him while riding, and that they were written in 'horse metre'. While singing them one is conscious of cantering or trotting. But the same creative process was at work on the preachers, and it did much to determine both the method and message of those early thinkers. This is not the place for a discussion on the psychology of riding, but having tried both the older and newer methods I have come to see that there is something in the very act of riding that is conducive to good conversation and creative thought. Whether it be the varying rhythm of the pattering hoofs, or that the blood is better disposed by motion in the whole body and every part made active, I know not. But certain it is that the whole organism is in a more eager disposition to serve its king, the mind. I would unhesitatingly favour riding for any one suffering from a sluggish mind, especially in a day when so much of the world's thinking has become mechanized, like the machines it is using. How much healthier mentally were our forefathers who enjoyed the poetry of riding! Dare I suggest their sermons were the better because of this health?

A FATAL FASCINATION

We were now only some thirty miles from home, and perhaps it was the salt sea tang in the air that told Dick he was heading for that desired place. But there were yet two other spots that had to be visited, and to visit them involved a circular tour. Just outside the incomparable little village of Langton I had the joy of meeting a middle-aged man I had seen under very different conditions on a previous tour. On that occasion he had been heavily under the influence of drink, and I had tried to reason with him about breaking the habit. He repaid my efforts with curses, and told me how his wife and children had all tried to persuade him against it. 'If I haven't listened to them, do you think I'm going to listen to you?' he almost hissed.

Why I replied as I did, I do not know, but I said, 'I don't want you to listen to me, I want you to see that it is not an accident that you and I have met, and that God is warning you through me that if you don't change, you are heading for a crash which will involve your wife and children as well as yourself.'

He swore, and staggered off down the road.

Yet here he was, just a year later, coming miles out of his way to thank me, and tell me of his change.

I remembered this man so well because just after leaving him I encountered a sight I had often wanted to see and which I associated with him. We were trotting around a corner keeping to the grass verge and had time to pull up so as not to disturb a scene as weird as it was unexpected. If both the figures in the drama had not been so preoccupied they would have vanished at our approach.

Half crouching in the middle of the road was a young hare—perhaps just past the leveret stage. It was gazing transfixed at a stoat. Sitting there in the saddle I watched one of the most fantastic sights I had ever witnessed.

The stoat was going round and round in circles as though it were chasing its own tail and pausing now and then to fix its fiery little eyes on the hare. Wildly circling round like a dancing dervish it was getting continually nearer to the hare. This senseless creature was so fascinated that it could not take away its eyes, even though its whole body was keyed up with tense apprehension.

Nearer, and still slowly nearer came the stoat, all the time keeping up its wild gyrations.

It was apparent that soon the fatal spring would take place. The scene was uncanny and murderous. All my sympathies were utterly with the helpless victim, and I determined at this stage to take a hand.

Urging Dick into a gallop we clattered into the road. The stoat immediately rushed into the hedge while the hare paused for a few dazed moments. During those moments I deliberately turned in between the hedge and the hare, thinking I would drive the hare the other way, but to my astonishment the hare deliberately ran into the hedge where the stoat had gone. There had been ample time for it to go in *any* direction, but it followed after the spellbinder!

It would be about fifteen minutes later as I sat eating some refreshment on a nearby gate top, that suddenly, from about one hundred yards away there came a most piteous squeal. The fascination had been fatal.

None of us like being warned. We all prefer the 'All clear' to the 'Take cover'. Nevertheless, it is sometimes necessary, and often the only method. Having warned the drunkard, I never thought I should see him again. I felt that the stoat would win. But one never knows what may happen when God has been given a chance.

DINSDALE T. YOUNG

To have lingered with him longer would have been a joy, but Scagglethorpe was my next destination. The invitation to come to this little wayside village had been eagerly seized because I knew of its association with Dr. Dinsdale T. Young. Sitting by the roadside and looking at that small chapel, originally built in 1816 as a private church, I recalled that it was here Dr. Young, as a boy of fifteen, had preached his first sermon.

When the time for service arrived we crowded into that little place. The occasion was unique. One could not refrain from reading the same lesson which had been read by that boy so many years ago, and preaching from the text he then used. *Seek ye the Lord while He may be found.* How fittingly that first text summarizes his subsequent great ministry that was to hold the heart of London for a quarter of a century. It has always been my conviction that a service should equip us for service, and that the test of a service is what happens when the congregation leave. After this service every one went visiting, and soon every one in every house in the place had been invited to join us on the village green. Here a service of witness was held, thanks largely to the keen support of a group of young people who had cycled in from the surrounding towns and villages. I feel sure the crowded church and the testimonies on the village green would have delighted the heart of Dinsdale Young.

THE VALLEY

My tour was drawing to a close when Dick and I set our course for Yeddingham.

A little place to-day, Yeddingham was once a thriving posting-station on the road to York. Now it is visited chiefly for its old bridge and the ruins of an abbey. The Vicar of Yeddingham has been a good friend to me more than once, and it was natural that I should make straight for his home. I may say that this good, energetic lover of souls had arranged everything beforehand, from the afternoon devotional service in the small church, to the crowded evening meeting in the Methodist chapel, where it was a joy and a privilege to share the platform with him.

And yet not quite everything had been arranged, for there was no one to ring the church bell for the afternoon service, with the result that I took the part of bellringer, quite a new experience. The vicar, however, said generously that he thought the whole journey had been one of bellringing, and perhaps in a way it had.

Little did either of us realize for whom the bell was calling. After the meetings I never saw this kindly man again, for shortly after this he retired for the night, and although apparently in the best of health, he never awakened. Nevertheless, the tolling of the bell in his own little church had, I am certain, been but the prelude to a mighty peal that greeted him on the other side.

SHADOW AND SUNSHINE

All good things come to an end, and presently I found myself riding through a valley which was to lead me home. Shadow and sunshine lay across my path, for there were great trees standing like giants between me and the low sun. I remember how in those last few miles I held a court of inquiry.

Had the journey really been worth while?

Had it accomplished anything?

In one sense, no doubt, these questions were unanswerable, but in another I thought I might venture to answer them humbly and sincerely. It seemed to me that every day I had been throwing pebbles into pools of human life. Often I had thrown the pebbles with the deliberate intention of creating nothing more than a disturbance, for any kind of disturbance is better than stagnation. How far the ripples had travelled or how great the disturbances had been, I could not know, and could hardly ever expect to know. But at any rate I was certain of one thing—that Christianity was still alive in the land, especially in country places.

Jogging along the homeward track I looked back over the experiences and incidents of the way, realizing that if my methods had sometimes been unconventional, so also were some of the forms of Christianity I had laid bare. Not everywhere had I found orthodoxy; and not every one I had met had readily displayed the cardinal Christian virtues; but often—very often—there had been glimpses of inner preciousness of spirit, hints of hidden gold, suggestions of a great longing for God and for the things of God.

My feelings and thoughts were symbolized by the road I was travelling, a road dappled with sunshine and shadow. The shadows reminded me that Dick Turpin and I were to part company within an hour; and at that moment I realized afresh how deeply attached a man may become to a horse. I did not wonder that John Wesley used to speak of his horses as his comrades.

The shadows spoke also of disappointments along the way, for the journey had not been one of unfailing triumph or of encouragement without discouragement. I had been lifted up in spirit and cast down in spirit; and I had met with men and women upon whose embittered lives (as it seemed) I had made no impression for good. Truly there were shadows across the 800 miles Dick and I had travelled.

But there was sunshine—and I thanked God for it.

There was sunshine, and it thrilled as it humbled me. I had seen a new light on many a face. I had seen lives lived in darkness come forth into the light of God's forgiveness. I had seen old causes started again with new vigour. I had been met everywhere by friends who had made me wondrously welcome. On the whole the miles had been aglow with sunshine, and how great a privilege it had been to ride in it, and to find so many kindly folk!

Yet this was not all. If I had failed to stir one heart or change one life or sow one seed in God's wide fields, of one thing at least I was certain—that my own faith had been richly renewed. I had found that journeying *with* the gospel had been to journey *into* it. By giving the gospel message to others I had been giving it afresh to my own soul. Riding homeward amid the sunshine and shadow I found my heart overflowing with gratitude, my soul gripped by a new certainty.

This thought also occurred to me: that there is a sense in which a minister (especially if he be in charge of a large and flourishing church) needs from time to time to escape from it for his own sake and for the sake of those to whom he ministers. Nothing is easier than to become 'church-bound'—to become so absorbed by organization, so caught up in the routine machinery of churchmanship, that one loses the vital breath of one's message and mission. Becoming 'church-bound' is as dangerous to a minister as becoming 'pot-bound' is dangerous (and, indeed, fatal) to a plant. So then (as I told myself smilingly when almost within sight of my journey's end) I had been a cavalry commando and had thereby been commanded anew by Calvary. Apart from anything any one else might have gained, the rider on horseback had at least refreshed his own soul.

But the chief thought in my mind and heart in those last moments was a desire to tell the Church again of its need to get back to the highways and byways, the crowded streets and lonely lanes where men and women toil and travel. Most of the men and women of our day do not come to church. Therefore the church must go to them. It is no use spending much time discussing ways and means, forming sub-committees, and gathering importantly round tables. Movement starts when some one *moves*, and I feel that the time has come for a new crusade. If only to-morrow a new order of Friars began tramping on foot or riding on horseback along our roads, or cleaving the skies with more modern methods but—all of them preaching Christ and Him crucified, what a surge of new life might come to old England, what smouldering ashes of idealism might glow again, what fresh Pentecosts we might see! Symbolically speaking we must get back into the saddle!

Our hearts must burn to reach the men and women of our day. Most of them are indifferent—or perhaps most of them are really waiting. Certain it is that we must not wait, and that we must not be indifferent to indifference. We must go forth and compel the wanderers to come in.

I parted at last from my faithful Dick. As I left him I glanced round, and there he stood on a clifftop enjoying a well earned rest. His head was erect, and his eyes were fixed upon a golden lane across the sea . . . a shining pathway to infinity.

May I leave you with this picture of new highways to great possibilities, hoping that they may call you as they called me?